Love

Storm

&

Family

Published by DBrockman Publishing

Love, Storms, and Family
Copyrights © Sabrina Stubbins 2010
All rights reserved. Printed in the United States of America. No part of this may be reproduced and or transmitted in any form or by any means without written permission by the author, except in the case of brief quotations embodied in critical articles and reviews. Contact:

DBrockman Publishing,
P.O Box 173208
Tampa, Fl 33672
dbpublisher@yahoo.com

Important
    The materials in this book represent the person of the author and not be applicable to all situations. Many circumstances appear similar, but differ in respects
    Each reader should use caution in applying any material contained in this book to his other specific circumstance, and should seek advice of an appropriate professional.
(Author's note: Use your common sense!)

Table of Content

Love

Wishing on a star 7
Hot and Wet 10
I Still Could Feel You 13
Unlike Any Other 15
Your Eyes 16
Every time 18

Storm

Cannot Love 21
I Cannot Breathe 26
Thinking of You 27
Special Love 29
I Miss You 31
Why 32
Nothing 34
No Man 35
Why Love 37
Blue Sky 39

Family

Momma and Daddy 41
My Son 45
Thank You 48
Myself 50
Runaway 52
Nothing 53

Acknowledgements ii
About The Author v

Love, Storm, & Family

Wishing on a star

I was wishing for a star and upon that star I found my dream.

That star was so high in the sky I had to climb as far as I could climb because I was wishing for that start.

Away from my star I found myself slipping away, but some how I found myself back to my star.

I was wishing for a life change and that put back on track.

I wish that my light will shine and I will grow into a perfection that I was born to be. I knew than and I know now that my wish on that star will help me understand my life as I should.

On this earth my wish is on that star.

Without you...

Who say I cannot live without you?

I know if I could breathe without air for a second, and my heartbeat would start to beat again, so I could live without.

I being without you would feel like the world is up against me. All I dream about is you, so being without, would take the joy away from me.

I have created a symbol for what we share. When I gaze into your eyes without appreciating the way that you lay me down. I would light up the world from the way you touch me.

Being without you would make me pass out like the dead rose pastels that have fallen from the rose, without me noticing that you're here with me.

I would always look forward to the long walks on the beach at night and in the mornings. Without you is being without the cold winters and my soul would be on its own, because I could no longer smile without you.

I would never know what happiness would really mean without you. I'd have reason to live without you, no reason to be who is without you.

You're my lover, my best friend and husband, so being without you would only make me keep the fire burning for you only.

Hot and Wet....

I'm hot and wet and was thinking that we could make some hot passionate love.

That's why I have a hot and wet present waiting just for you.

I can see that you're hot and wet to, so let me give you a hint.

Do you know or do you want to know what it will involve?

It involves me and you, and the quite storm and a real quiet evening for the both of us.

You do not have to wait anymore. Come to my room and let me undress you, so you could feel how hot and wet am.

Do you like what I had in store for you?

Please can you touch me there????

You're always here with me, and you always seem to be in my dreams, and I always get weak at the knees when I fine myself savoring every kiss that you give.

My desire only waken me as I feel for you're lips. I like the feeling when you press your warm lips up against my flesh...

Except for that one special spot, which no one should press against, but you.

I only ask that you touch that spot when I am hot for you.

I may say later, but I have to say touch me now. Please can you touch me there????

I still could feel you...

You're always so far away, but so near, I still could feel you.

You are in every breath that I take. You're in every beat of my pulse, you're adding a sizzle to that warm place that you to touch so much.

When I close my eyes, I still could feel you as if you were still here. I'm so hot for you it feels just like a fire that is still burning.

You're presence is so unbelievable ......

Yet it is so hard to grasp that I could still feel you. I reach for you, but you're not there, but I still feel you as if you were still there.

I just want to feel the touch of your hands on my cheek, on my body.

A vision in my mind always comes back to you, because you're at a distant that a light can not see.

The ray of the sun brings you near to me.

Unlike any other....

I wanted to send you sex in the mail that speaks from my heart unlike any other, I want to tell you how you make feel.

I love you. I have never loved anyone like I love you.

The words that I speak are not strong enough to express how you're sex make me feel. I am deeply in love with you.

I can only say that you're my friend my lover and the love of my life.

The greatest dream that I have and want to come true is being your wife for life.

But to convey the sex that is so good and hot there's only one thing I can do; for the rest of my life is give it to you like any other women that had you.

You're Eyes

Can you take a ride with me, because your eyes are driving me crazy?

Can you take a ride with me, so I could do something to you that your women won't do to you?

See I am the type of girl that won't mess up your life, because I'll be real with you because I am not shy. See these bitches out here are lame.

I spit it real to your ass, because I shift gears in Chevy like am in a plane. I'll take yo ass head over heels.

I am in between your legs. I will have you moaning. You go to sleep and I wake you up and steel you want more of me. I cannot help it boy it's the love game that I have.

I cannot help it boo, my heartbeat and the blood running in my veins. I am not any bitch and I am not a scrub. I want to rub on your body boy while you're in the shower, kiss you all over your body like yo women should.

Shit doesn't that sounds good? Can you take a ride with me? Because your eyes driving me crazy.

Boy yo eyes are something like a drug, because I just want to do some freaky things to you that I can only dream of.

I am not trying to be yo women I am just trying to spend a little time with you and spend the night. It's a bet that I am grantee to do your body right.

I know you done heard how I put it down. You know that they call me Ms. Jackson cause I put it down like it's hot. No other women could do you I can.

YOUR EYES DRIVE ME CRAZY.

Every Time...

Every time I think of you, I think back to the time when we first meet.

Every time I think about you I think about the first kiss you gave me.

Every time I think about you I think about the first time we made love.

Every time I think about you I think about how you make me feel.

Every time I think about you I think about the stars that I see in your eyes.

Every time I think about you I think about the smile that you have.

Every time I think about you I think about the way you touch me.

Every time I think about you I think about the way that you hold me in your arms.

Every time I think about you I think about the ocean and the sea because that's how deep my love goes.

Every time I think of you it brings me to tears in because I think of you.
Every time

Can not love

I am sorry I can not love you.

I have tied my hardest to love you, but it failed.

So now my heart is closing its door.

So I can not get hurt again.

You said that you would stay on the same page, but you skipped a page on me.

Was my love good enough or was the problem me?

I am okay because I have found a place to put my heart.

I am done with waiting for love to come to me.

I am really listening to the man above.

He has given me the words to a song.

We were never mint to be, but I had to have you.

I put every thing into you to find out by loving you have hurt me.

I was alone until I meet you, but now I am letting you go so I could set myself free from you.

This time my heart will be filled with love and not with pain.

I am gone and I will not be back, I am gone forever.

I am sorry that I could not find your heart beat.

I am so sorry that we will never be together and I am sorry that you feel the pain too, but now you see how I hurt.

I was happy until I meet you.

Now I am happy without you.

I hope that you could see that my heart is beating again, but not for you.

This is something that I feel and I know that it is right.

When I stop loving you, I forgot how to love.

I use to be stupid in love with you.

I really thought it would work.

I really actually thought we would always last.

I am sorry to say I do not even love you anymore.

I can not love you.

I just can not love you anymore free is saying my name.

I know that I have to close my door.

I can not love you anymore.

I am so tied....

I am so tied of all the hurt.

I am tied of all the pain.

I am so tied of love pain that men bring to women.

I am so tied of love pain I have endure with the games that men play.

I am so tied of fighting this battle alone.

When it was over I relocated.

See, but I can not let it go, because people go through trails and tribulation and relationships do get better.

They say what can hurt you will only make you stronger and wiser.

I am tied of crying, so the tears, I am leaving behind is a trail for you to find your way back to me.

My dad and mom told me when I cry tears it only makes me want to love you more.

I am tied of sitting around waiting

for you to come back to me, but that is what loves all about a waiting game.

I have cried for you boy, but it is not doing any good because I still think of you and I being together.

I am tied of telling you this much is too much for more.

I am so tied of missing my hugs and kisses from you.

I tied of catching the movies.

I am so tied of being last in your life and I be D.A.M if I lose you.

I am so tied of your lies.

I am so tied of staying up late at night waiting for you to come home.

I am so tied of sitting here complaining to myself

I am so tied.

I can not breathe

One day in your life you will fine someone that will make you stop breathing. I was so in love and it made me stop breathing and he told me he would be on call me until I breathe again.

He said that when the world has me tripping he would be there to catch me when I fall.

He told that the world have me tripping he will be there to catch me when I fall.

When nightfall comes he say to me let me return you to your bed, so I could give you my devoted attention until I start breathing.

Until my heart start beating rest your head upon my chest and it will help you to understand, that we are one and not two, but without you I can not breathe. Without you are so cold and I am crying out to you that I love you. At less until I start breathing.

I think of you....

I think of you everyday.

I think of you when I am a lone.

I think of you when I am lying in my bed when your not there.

I think of you when I am in the shower.

I think of you when it's raining.

I think of you when their colds because I could feel your body up against me, DAM how I wish you were near.

I think of you when I am looking up in the sky.

I think of you when I am having wine and listing to music.

I think of you when I see a SHOOTING STAR fall from the sky.

I think of you when I see a rainbow in the sky because it reminds me of how cheerful you are when we are together.

I think of you when I think about how happy you have made me in the years that have passed and the years to come, and the years that we have started in our new life.

    I think of you everyday Boo.

    When I think of you it comes from the bottom of my heart.

    That's how much I think of you Boo.

Special Love

I fell in love when I looked in your brown eyes.

I fell in love with you when you kiss me.

I fell in love with you and you took my heart away.

I fell in love with you because of your smile.

I fell in love with during the summer of 99.

I fell in love with you because you gave me a high.

I fell in love because of the way you think.

I fell in love with because I was told that we were mint to be...

I fell in love with you because I knew that you would be by my side.

I fell in love with you because I knew that there was no other for me.

I fell in love because you're my best

friend.

I fell in love with you because of the way you touched me.

I fell in love with you because I KNEW WITH YOU IT WAS REAL AND NOT A DREAM.

I fell in love with you because I knew it will never end.

I fell in with you so we could fall in love a gain.

I fell in love with you because it felted like my first time.

I fell in love with you because I know that you would not forget about me.

I fell in love with you because your touch is a powerful thing.

I fell in love with you.

I miss you....

I miss you're warm touch, the way that you hold me.

I miss you're soft lips. I miss the way you kiss me all over.

I miss the way you rub you're tongue up against my body and the moments that we share together in our bed.

I miss the love making that we do in the evening when we are a lone.

I miss you.

I always look forward to the nights, because knowing that, it makes the nights closer to you being in our bed.

You must have known that you're my king and that I miss you dearly... I MISS YOU...

Why....

He said why he loves me.

He said why he cares for me.

He said why he should call me.

He said why I should be there to catch her when she falls.

Why should I give her my shoulder to cry on?

He said that I am just stuck in the world.

He said the world is just a place where it could just chew you up and spit you out.

He said why I should leave my heart cold and in pain.

I thought I knew about love.

He said that he really thought he loved her, but I guess that he did not.

He was wrong.

He said why I even can not be friends with her?

He said why I SHOULD be NICE to

her.

He said why I should let her call me N.A.M.E.S like fuck nigga.

So now why should I pray for her?

Nothing

I was nothing, but I have so long ago turned into something that I have always wanted to become and that is peace within me.

Although that nothing sometimes appear once in a while, I P.U.S.H IT AWAY.

When nothing comes back I put myself back at peace where I should be.

When I am at peace I could feel the wind, the sun and the rain, and the cold.

When I feel that I feel the women within me.

If it was not for nothing I would not be the woman am today.

No MAN

No man is truly loved, until he understands every word his love is not saying.

They will never know true love are happiness until they have truly loved, and he will never understand what pain is all about, until he loses everything.

For man to live is to love his life, but for some reason he do not have one.

He has to hold it against all healthy instinct for it will come together for the better of love.

True love can be found, but to man it truly do not exist, nor, can it be found in their heart.

TO MAN LOVE IS A TEMPORARY FIX, BECAUSE THEY FEEL IS NOT REAL.

For man to be in love it merely something that they will share.

It's almost like a strong stage of a

forbidden fruit that they can not have.

To mistake an ordinary man for god, it would be like life of a death sentence.

So men know that the tree will not blossom, without a tree that the fruit of love do not exist.

Why Love

Why love to be hard?

Why love fails you?

Why love can not be easy?

Why loves cause you to fight?

Why love makes you said sometimes?

Why love makes you shut down?

Why love always keeps two people together when they're not mint to be?

Why love uses your heart?

Why love takes your breath away from you?

Why love does not have a voice when it comes to love?

Why love brings two people together?

Why love does not have an understanding?

Why love is pain?

Why love is pleasure?

Why have a special feeling?

Why have a fairy tail ending?
Why love leafs fall from the tree?
Why love always has around it?
Why love makes you cry?
Why must you understand love?
You must love to understand the meaning of love.

Blue Sky

Blue sky where are you?

Blue where are you?

You know that I need you.

Blue sky is you going to let me find you?

Blue sky when are you going to come?

Blue sky when are you going to show me that you're concern about me.

Blue sky I need you to shine your light upon me like you use to.

Blue sky I need you to come out of the dark to shine your light that you have over me, so the angel could find me.

Blue sky does not go through the blackness on me.

Blue sky I am lost without you in my life.

Blue sky I need you really, really need you bad, how can I find you?

Blue sky please make me happy like you use to, so I could shine again.

Blue sky where are you?

Family

Momma and Daddy

On March 4, 1967 I was born to Delores Pelham (Collins) and Willie Crumpler.

Momma and Daddy said that I was a dreamer, but I made my dreams come to reality and I am showing you momma and daddy that I did it.

When things were getting heavy for me momma and daddy you were there to pick me up.

See momma you and Daddy raised me in a good home with morals, so I made you and Daddy proud of me by getting my degree. I work real hard for it.

I was all by myself 38 years old you and Daddy knew that I was a loner because I was the only girl and the oldest of our family.

I am a black woman of static's and 40 years old and I was a victim of momma and daddy trying to show me the right way before it was to late.

Momma and Daddy you pushed so I would not be pushed into the states hands. They showed me how to push myself so I could be recognized by words and mot by face.

What they thought me was to know right from wrong, so I will not end up dead or in jail.

Momma and Daddy thought me the game when I was little and that was how to write my name and that lead me to write poetry. They asked me what I wanted to be when I grow up, I said forget about being a dancers or a singer, or a teacher I want to be an poet, that was my interdiction to me writing poetry when I was taught how to write my name, they said that I will go places, so now I see that they really noticed the talent that I have in me.

Momma and Daddy said that my

poetry could write its own convictions
and that I would have sold out shows
and I will be winner.

    Momma and Daddy I have made
you and daddy a heart and I wrote in it (I
MADE IT).

    Momma and Daddy I made it.

    Momma and Daddy 10 or 15 years
later I made it.

    Momma and Daddy only saw the
good in me so they were my fan base and
they were the only one who knew that
will proper if I tied

    I was raised in the project so I
knew what I was up against. I was so
content but I had to try and stay focus
against the battle of the world.

    To the current events, and my
momma and daddy ain't nothing change
but me wishing for my future to change.

    My rent was do and I was told to
get off my ass and get a job or go to

school so you could have money to pay your rent. So I went back to school, so momma and daddy I told them one day I will have my own business and its coming soon.
I have faith.

My Son

My son I know you have seen a lot of things and you have had some sunny days and you have endure some pain and son I know you have had lots of days running away from a lot things in your life.

Son the lord have blessed you in some many ways, but you just do not want to do right and take what G.O.D have given you, so he showed you who was B.O.S.S.

I am just thankful that G.O.D kept you here with me baby boy, now you got to change your ways, because the lord have given so many chances to C.H.A.N.G.E Y.O.U.R L.I.F.E.

So that means no more sitting in the trap running from the police. I know that you could change because you're not one that sits on your ass; you're a real go-getter.

See your still a live and your so lucky because you know where your from they are K.I.L.L.I.N.G young men you're A.G.E.

Son you have bad habits and you need to let them go, you have already been to jail and prison, so let it go.

So you need to be trying to into H.A.V.E.N and not into H.E.L.L

The lord know what you have been through every time you have tried to change you always fine yourself back with them friends and they do not even give a D.A.M about you.

I know you're out there hustling because you're tied of being broke, and tied of struggling, and I know every time you close your eyes you're praying to the lord for a better day.

I know when your sleep you dream of a better life for your daughter and yourself.

I know you're tied of seeing broke days. I know your starving for money son, so you try get at any means, so you hit the block because that's what you know.

Son in life you have to choose your path and ask the lord to show you the way.

So all I want is the best for you leave that life alone and live the life that you need for your child M.Y. S.O.N

Thank You……

Thank you Dad for my health and my strength and thanks for encouraging me to go to collage.

Thank you dad for the activity of my limbs.

Thank you dad for my family near and far, but most of all dad I have to praise you for the person that you are.

Dad it's the mist of darkness that you are my G.O.D, and that you are my dad.

Dad, you are my day and my night, so I take this time to say THANK YOU for being my DAD.

Thank you dad for what you have made of me and for what you have made of yourself and what I have made of myself.

Thank you dad for what you have done for me.

Thank you dad for the food you

have given me to eat.

Thank you dad for giving me a warm place to sleep.

Thank you dad for being precious to me.

Thank you dad for loving me and seeing a wretch like me.

When I started to weigh the things that you have done for me they will tip over the scale, especially the things you have given me and how you have save my soul from the burning hell.

So now I take this my time by saying THANK YOU again DAD for what you have done for me and getting me through the years that was not so great.

Thank You Dad.

Dad I love you.

Myself

I see myself in the mirror, and I see a reflection of myself.

I do not know whether I should laugh or cry. I just do not know which one it should be.

The reflections that I see of me go on until there is no end.

Am really a strong person and I am very still inside.

I want to cry but am all cried out. The confusion in my mind will not let me go; they always keep me behind these walls.

Mirror, mirror, mirror, mirror please tell me that I will someday see myself.

I will be strong so I will try not to cry, so I want leave these tears behind. If I cover it up in my mind tell me what will I see?

Will I see my reflection of me and if I do I will not like what I see in the reflection of me.

Therefore I am not important, so yes indeed I am a mirror of my own reflection.

Run Away

Run away from your fears.

Hide behind your tears.

Do not let him see what you really feel inside, dry your eyes.

You do not have to hide.

Run away from the rain and hide from the sun.

He will never think to find you here at the place that despises the fear that you have within yourself.

That just too much fear that you have inside of you.

Run away from pain that lives in someone else's life.

I do not think that I will ever be able to transform and live my life.

I would die and become someone else because that's where the new life begins because no one ever wanted to me.

Nothing

I was nothing, but I have so long ago turned into something that I have always wanted to become and that is peace within me.

Although that nothing sometimes appear once in a while, I P.U.S.H IT AWAY.

When nothing comes back I put myself back at peace where I should be.

When I am at peace I could feel the wind, the sun and the rain, and the cold.

When I feel that I feel the women within me.

If it was not for nothing I would not be the woman I am today.

THE ...... END

i

Acknowledgement

I'm deeply grateful for the time and energy, love and prayers of those who supported me while I was writing my 2 poetry books.

I will like to thank the above for so much support in my writing these 2 books. I will like to thank Dexter Brockman for giving me these chances to write these books and believing in me. Thank you Dexter for your support.

To my children and my unborn grandson and to my other unborn grandchild, and Sha sha, Sariaha, and my daughter-n-law Kyla and her children. My mom my father, and step father and stepmother. I want to that all of you for providing me with the strength in which these lessons have been tested. I have prayed that I finish what I set out to do in my life and I have thanks to you all that is in my life, and I hope in years to come my poetry will be passed on to my grandchildren and I hope that they have the same talent that I have in writing, and in poetry. Trust me if they are anything like me they will have the passion for writing and anything else that their hearts desirer. My passion of writing will be a message of my trust and precious gift that will not be taken for granted.

I know that my children or grandchildren will do something it.

A special thanks to Derick and Minnie Williams for being there with me though it all. Thanks you for the Angel you put into my life. Love you Mrs. Minnie Williams.

I send my Love to every one that show me love thought out me writing my book.

Things that are in my book are true and some or not. It up to you to determine which or true if you choose to.

Thank you for buying my book. I hope that it could help you with your family, your love life, and in the romance department. Thanks to all who have brought my book. Sabrina.

ABOUT ME

Family: Family is the most important thing in the world to me.

I will like to thank my family for being in my life when I was at my lowest point in my life.

I will like to thank the old MIGHTY GOD, my mom Delores Collins, my father Willie Crumpler. I many are wondering why my name is spelled different. On my dad mom had missed spelled it, but later on my dad had his last name change to his father last name and that was Crumpler. My mom and dad are the best parents that any child could ever wish for. Mom and Dad I love both until

I will like to thank my step- parents for being for me too:

Lorenzo Collins: is the best step-father that a girl or women could ever ask for. He is a strong man and when you need him he is the type of person will be there when you can. I love you very much. I'm glad that you're in my life.

Elizabeth Crumpler.: My momma and my friend when I needed her she was there for me. She is the type of person that will give you the shirt off her back. I love you so much.

To my Children: Lopez Hearns, Talesha Crumpton, and Marquita Hearns: When GOD gave you all to me that could have been the best thing that he could have ever gave. I love you guys so much. When the wind blows by you all remember it is just me looking over you guys to keep you all safe from harm.

To my grandchildren's and that mean my step grandchildren too. I love you all so much.

To my daughter - law: I'm glad that you are in my son's life. I also what you to know that I love you as if you were my own. I love you.

www.ingramcontent.com/pod-product-compliance
Lightning Source LLC
Chambersburg PA
CBHW032017290426
44109CB00013B/698